Witness

Witness

Poems by

John Peter Harn

Cover design by Shay Culligan

Cover photograph by Michelle Harn
"Evergreen Cemetry, Galveston"

Author Photograph by Etsuko Matsunaga

ISBN: 978-1-950462-41-4

Kelsay Books Inc.

kelsaybooks.com

502 S 1040 E, A119
American Fork, Utah 84003

for

Emily Rachel
Etsuko
Jessica Aya
and
Michelle Megumi

my family

and

Cindy Veach, Carol Durak
Michael Malan and Brad Maxfield

for reading many of these poems in their early stages

Acknowledgments

Chicago Quarterly Review: "In December '44, in the Ardennes"

DMQ Review: "Words I Don't Know"

Miramar: "Although Much is Implied"

New Orleans Review: "What to Expect of the Decades"

Red Rock Review: "Not once in a decade"

Spillway: "Street Vendor Florist"

Contents

IV Decades

I

Galveston Suite

it took a while to care again
what happened in the world of people

Evergreen Cemetery, Galveston Island

No one, lowering their dear departed
into the ground on straps
laying them to rest in the last century
saw this coming
these wildflowers, this orange blanket
cozying up, lapping stones
the whole long stretch of this place
ankle-deep in bloom
following the lay of the land
reaching for the daytime moon.

And yet, it does seem predictable
this place would fall on hard times
abandoned, unloved
that the earth would bathe it once a year
in a fleeting grace
and mottled stones would lend their perfect grey.

Still, I'm sure
no one back then saw this coming.
Not the builders with their iron gate and sad Madonna
not the bereaved, tethered to clergy, plowing grief,

which is why I pull over
get out and walk around.
To tell everyone
how things turned out
to stroll and sit and waste my time
giving updates to the dead.

Me and Oleander

A Sunday morning church bell passes
through me and oleander.

I'm sunning on the little balcony
outside my front door
resting in god's good graces
when one-by-one, up and down my quiet street
blasphemers awake
rustle and shout
smack tools and start engines
slashing their unending
weekend to-do lists.

Dogs bark, unchastised.
Radio ads storm the lulls.
A hammer pounds what's left
of morning into dust.

> *What roadblock let this hunger pass*
> *what bottleneck this thirst.*

People should be more like lizards.
If a fly lands
while they're sunning
nothing happens.

View from a Collapsible Beach Chair

Salt decides
how long things last.

Pelicans fold
dive and steal.
Seagulls hijack and escape.

And people come here too
from far away
     to beachcomb their ancestry
     wade in the abyss
     catch a glimpse of themselves from above
         pissing away their minuscule investments.

The sweet smell of sulfur
rises off seaweed.

Another day
plucked from
returned to.
Held and let go.

Archived in the Waves

Almost every day I walk the beach
to keep my heart
the organ going.

No one makes a living
listening to waves anymore.

I remember my first envelopment.
Nine or ten years old
holding a dead dragonfly by the tail
lost in fluorescent wings and alien eyes

an expanding self-absence descended.

It took a while to care again
what happened in the world of people.

Last night I dreamed my grandfather
gone fifty years, waited in a room to surprise me.
When I opened the door, we ran to each other
laughing, crying, planting soft kisses
on each other's bristled cheeks.

What *isn't* archived in the waves
might be a better question.

December 31st

No one invited the solstice
to the New Year's Eve party
on Galveston Island's balmy East Beach
so I appointed myself
emissary, telling any who'd listen
the truth about when
a new year begins.

Normal people don't care
about a planet's absolutes.
They're busy shining
wherever live music meets a cash bar
they're content to drink and dance and feel the Gulf
push perfume over the island.

Not everyone needs
to pull the wrapper off.
Not everyone is a sanctuary.
How many can carry
their weight around in grace.

Some stars poke through
party lights and tiki torches.
The surf's a perfect backdrop
for cover tunes, idle chatter
and dancers feeling lucky on a cramped dance floor.

And so my tribe gathers
in the debris field of love and lives lost
to put their faith in the coming new year
ten days late on purpose.

Palms and Explode

I'm checking off a list of things
I'm willing to forget
like footprints on the moon
true north
love's dandelion runway.

It's a long list
and some things don't want to give up
the high ground, but they will.

The clang and ping of a soda can
replaces a lullaby.
A stray dog's wag replaces
a child's hand in a crosswalk.

Some midnight, years from now
I'll put what's left in a rucksack
arc out over coconut palms
and explode above the Gulf
like a firework returning
the thump it borrowed from black.

But for now, I have this list
that needs my eye
and a sun that needs review
so I'll keep casting
rust into wind.

Laughable, Inadequate

They say the heat here
breaks people in summer.

I'm counting on that.

I plan to be dozing when the worst of it comes
woefully unprepared
like Columbus in the crow's nest
drunk, run aground.

I'll deploy a theory of heat at first
laughable, inadequate, to buy time.
But I'll surrender when the exotics march in.

> *Dragonflies and blue agave*
> *dive-bombing each other's fertility.*

> *Invasive birds in the wrong eggshells.*

> *The historic mural at city hall*
> *flashing its erotic under-sketch.*

Ninety-nine
degrees at midnight.
My house a banyan tree.
Poems hang like gourds in the afterlife.

Sunday in Galveston

means coffee on the Strand.

Tourists stroll antique shops and galleries
moving slow in the heat
trying to rekindle
lantern soot and lace.

The sun gets stuck
plowing main street
and we broil.

Wooden signs over storefronts
creak in code.

A brick wall reveals
it's drowned and been revived.

> *At the beach, my grown daughter*
> *visiting for summer*
> *pushes through breakers for a swim.*
> *She goes in to be moved by swells.*
> *She comes out strung with pearls.*

Sunday on the island.
Peak heat.
Dozing in the torrent of now.

Yes, I'll say it out loud

in front of everyone,

Oh, to be a bird!

despite the Jonathan Livingston
Seagull thing
because just look
into the eye of a bird

up close if you can

for as long as you can

any bird… take your time…

Do you feel an inverted logic fanning out?
Does a small blue flame pop up between you?
Can you sense some new antiquity
alive the world?

So why shouldn't I
say it out loud,

Oh, to be a bird,

and then, under my breath, so no one else hears,

and for that bird to be me…

Over on the mainland

skyscrapers sweep
acres of cloned corn
while dams, linked by a daisy chain
of high-voltage razor wire,
pass stolen cash from coast to coast.

Which is exactly why
I'm on this island instead
just offshore
under new management
on excellent terms with gulls and salt grasses.

There are vacancies here
for the idle
mangoes for the homeless
echoes of the oldest
dreams in the waves.

Cross-legged in the shadow of a coconut palm
I'm doing god's work
merging English words with a light rain's patter.

Padded Basket

Midnight. Wet streets.
A voice but not a voice
hangs like a tendril from a gargoyle oak.

There's a lament up in the branches.

It's a boy I think, sung-to just once
unnamed and left
in the perpetual care of the ages.

He needs but can't need
seeks but can't seek.

Dear god-of-things-like-this
let me be his padded basket tonight.
Let him feel what love I have
for him before it passes.

The swish of a nearby heart
was once his near and far.
It was a lot
but not enough.

Words I Don't Know

A cold north wind
strips the beach this morning
calm by noon
then a sweltering end.

When a day lasts a year, like this one
I'm compelled to remember the old ones
here before us
a woman, a baby, a basket of fish
men bending rush
into thatch.

I squeeze water from a handful of wet sand.
Words I don't know
stick to my palm
songs I don't know
fall out of the waves.

Out in the oyster beds, silt self-replicates.
Pearls strung and unstrung.

At the beach

a toddler feels the earth sucked out
from under her feet by waves

a dim old woman sees a thousand miles

a man hears his eulogy
recanted in the waves.

At the beach
everyone knows what the cosmos wants

what matters
what doesn't
how it all ends.

II

Sticky Notes to Self

when I started climbing trees
I stopped choosing sides

Sticky Notes to Self

*

None of the illuminations
tucked in the secret lining of your sarcophagus
will help you in the afterlife.

*

Despite your claims to the contrary
you don't actually know
what happens inside a leaf
seconds before a downpour.

*

Why not let the slate
stay blank for once.
Why force yourself
to pull it behind you like a rickshaw.

*

When I started climbing trees
I stopped choosing sides.

*

Everyone's book of lore
bleeds out in the end
pulled downriver and back out to sea.

*

Your theory is intriguing.
Keep it in a cool dark place
while you fabricate some evidence.

Geography Quiz, with Answers

Where's the best place to fly over
in a one-man glider
climb out on a wing and drop
a thousand little questions tied up in string.

The bend in the river, where it all began.

*

And where's the best place to be vacant
to twang a guitar string and feel
the vibration fade and nothing take its place.

The wormhole at the center of a sunflower.

*

And where's the best place to give up the ghost
hoist it up a flagpole
dust off your hands, salute and walk away.

On a grassy hill, plied by wind.

*

And where's the best place to wake up
in the coma of your first long kiss
lost inside that kind of percussion.

Up on the roof, where little feet skip by.

Arithmetic

If a barn door is torn off
and sent sailing in a squall
never to be seen again
       it means all is well
       with the falling together and the flying apart.

      *

And if, no matter where you stand, sit, kneel or lie
a giant sequoia won't fit
in your camera's viewfinder
       move back until it does.
       Build a perch to watch and wonder from.

      *

And if, walking nowhere special
a broken sidewalk carries you
to a crumbled foundation
       it means what's followed you
       has caught up.

Cuttings

for Dru Sensei

A full moon hangs from a fishing line
above the Gulf.
White shells tussle in the surf.
Four kinds of clouds.

*

A gecko suns itself
on a marble buddha's pregnant ear.
Trickling water lets it
sleep there all day.

*

Rubble on the desert floor.
Obsidian, pumice, fossil bone.
Once this was a forest
now, star-shine and crunch.

Way Past Due

Everyone wants to see a tall ship
go down bravely in a storm.
        Ask a statistician
        when and where to stand.

        *

A tin roof protects you
from the cosmos' brutal rain
        but you're way past due
        to be carried off in a storm.

        *

Not even a gothic cathedral
stays out of the scrap heap forever.
        Sacred light
        finds its limit.

III

A Hundred Disposable Distractions

*when plus and minus swap poles
we'll need new words for everything*

A Hundred Disposable Distractions

*

If we could ascend
vertically up

if there were enough lift for us
to rise indefinitely

would a braided stream of our cells stretch back
to earth

and if we kept that tether
plush and maintained it
no matter how far we went
or what we found
if we stayed connected
to where we were conceived

what would become of us
out there in the dark

what colors would we find
in the eddy reaching back

what shapes
in as far as the eye can see.

*

Ten pm
candlelight
a piano seeps
up through floorboards from the apartment below.

Ah, to be transported
from nowhere to nowhere else.

The shells and leaves I keep on a shelf
to remind me what I am
the acorns and pinecones I've borrowed for now
join me in a fleet migration of keys.

*

An over-ripe fig
hangs like bruised meat
from a fifty-year-old branch
food for wasps and ants.

I found it by accident
following a hedgerow laid down
by a clan no one knows
the name of anymore.

The earth rises up.
The branch dips down.
The fig won't ask
more favors of the dirt.

*

My friend likes to riff
about the spiritual underpinnings
of abstraction.

I thought of him last night
out for a walk
when an iridescent ring of ice
encircled the full moon
big enough to hold
a hundred moons inside it.

That's the kind of sovereignty he'd like
up there in the frozen layers
adrift, aloft,
hobnobbing with the other
free electrons in heaven.

*

A man, holding onto his hat
chases his aesthetic down a windy street
but both get away from him.

How much easier it would be
if he saw nothing but
what he chased after
and all else were blurred
if he saw it from a distance at first
getting closer as he closed the gap
until he could at some point
just reach out and grab it.

His conundrum is like
what to do with the tainted food
left out all night after a party
when everyone wakes up
the next day starving.

*

He set his alarm
so his dream could start
an hour before dawn.

He got up, got dressed
and climbed down to the beach in the dark
to watch the sun rise over the Gulf.

It rowed in on a calling card
sizzled in a pan
hitched a ride on rails back around.

It was hard for him to wake up
in the dark and get dressed
and not fall down the embankment

but now he knows
what happens in his sleep.

*

He thought the end when it came
would be beautiful somehow
like a tropical sunset
or a mountain of familial love
or a close-up view of Saturn whizzing by.

It never occurred to him
he'd be trying to feed
bills into a subway ticket machine
that the air would be stale
and the ground would rise up
not with the whispering green
new testament on its breath
but the taste of blood and the smell of concrete.

*

In the middle of the floor
in a gallery exhibiting
Dutch masters
a chunk of broken concrete
some dust and some pieces.

A family of four from Des Moines
makes a circle around it.

They look up at the ceiling
    but it's black and shows nothing
they look at the walls
    but they're completely self-absorbed.

No one can say
how long they stood there
in the ear-like curl of their question.

Driving home the usual
fast-food signs flew by
but they didn't have that
kind of hunger anymore.

*

A ten-year-old girl
crawls into a conch shell
and won't come out.
She has some questions about the why of it.

Twenty people can tell her
how it came to be
but that's not what she's after this time.

Her fingers try to see
beyond its ingenious horizon.

It has no smell
unless distance is a smell.

She hears the background hiss
when it's up to her ear.

She passes the weight of it
from hand to hand.
In the left, ancestral heft,
something more intended in the right.

Alone in the fog of her war
she hasn't washed up
on any shore just yet.
But she's mastered being ten.

*

He carries faded stains
of indelible things.

    Sitting on a terrycloth towel
      at a public pool
        eating ice cream on a stick.

    Lying on a neighbor's lawn
      watching clouds
      watching clouds.

    Tossing a phone number
      out a speeding car window
      a flutter in the rear-view mirror.

Heavy metals streak
seams of marble blue.

*

Think of it as a tightrope
a foot off the ground.
Step on or step off
or pay it no mind.

Or think of it as Godzilla
taking a breather on an overturned building
having coffee and croissant
brushing away flies.

> *If a dew-dotted web moves in and out of focus*
> *if a curl of steam offers you a handle*
> *if ice crystals spread like a cherished disease*
> *you too could drip*
> *like blood into snow.*

*

I'm taking my sweet time
pawing through the pile of stuff
leftover from last year
rooting and sifting and following the trail
of pigment back to its source.

I find an abandoned house
on a dried-up lot.
Faded advert stuck in its fence
its gravel driveway now a part of the soil.

Out back, out of reach
of my naked eye
wagon ruts arc east.

*

He knows all about
the daydreaming loophole.

He stares through his reflection
in a moving train window
projects himself onto
what's around the next bend.

Earlier, shaving in a steamy
bathroom mirror
he saw the unfolding
scene he was in
had been recycled a thousand times.

He was elated
he was scared
and those were recycled too.

*

Which is better
the back of the hand
with its rivers and mountains and ancestral bone
or the palm
with its valleys and alleys and treasure X.

If I examined your hands
slow as continental drift
turning them over
front to back, back to front
if I called in all my IOUs

what seawall would I find
against what shore.
Which mooring.
Which you.

*

At a four-way stop in the middle of nowhere
four cars are waiting
to see who goes first.

One with a bashed up
little ego.

One with a girl in the passenger seat
cupping her hands in her lap.

One that's reeling in the FM vibes

and one whose driver is very far away
wondering why Picasso's head exploded
in Paris, not Spain.

A crow watches from a streetlight.
When no one moves
it flies off, ticked off.

*

In Catholic school, nuns committed
countless acts of science.

Seashells in the alps.
The reproductive system of worms.
The circadian rhythm we share
with the rest of the biosphere.

Oh, the heat they must have prayed in
kneeling at the feet of their beds
begging forgiveness for the fossil record.

For accidentally brushing
another sister's hand in the kitchen
they prayed extra.
As if there were so many
hours in a day.

*

Once,
giant cedars roamed here
vascular and cycling
centuries through the understory

and before them it was ice
discharging in meltwater
all the syllables we have today

and before ice it was basalt
filling in cracks
smoothing things over
leaving puzzles in the grain

but now a suburban split-level is here
with a moss-free roof
where a ninth-grade girl is
doing homework in a room
with glow-in-the-dark stars on the ceiling.

Outside,
beyond the reach of her reading light
in the woods between
her window and the school bus stop
an hour-hand cradles a minute-hand
under sycamore leaves.

*

     For my eyes, a rainbow arcs
off the earth like a solar flare.

     For my ears, the chatter-hiss
of a stream's conversation with moss.

     For my skin, her fingerprints on mine
and the endless loop of her long hair.

     For my mind, morning sun in the room we let
overlooking the bridge of sighs.

*

Some people can't bear
the sound of traffic noise.
If a truck rumbles, too close
they die within days
and no one knows why.

Out in the Oort Cloud
in the belly of *Voyager*
stowaways wait.
Mitosis, suspended.
Silence, frozen.
The sun is just a star.

*

Half the world hibernates
face-down in a cracked illusion.

If someone thinks the sun sets everywhere at once
then the sun sets everywhere at once.

Contrails stitch tartan skies together.
The sun bounces once before setting.

When plus and minus swap poles
we'll need new words for everything.

*

A screen door, pulled by a spring
slams under a yellow porch light.

A dog bark washes in
from the next county.
Cicadas. Wind in the corn.

Upstairs, in a darkened sick-room
horse tack hangs
from rafters in the back
of old man Schneider's mind.

*

He comes home from work
and greets his spinning dog in the foyer.
Dust corkscrews in a shaft of sunlight.

It's not just locomotives
fused in a head-on crash
that kills me.
Not just iron shot into fury.
It's the small conversions too
the heat the bed
gives up when we rise
the scratch that sloughs off a universe
every scent requires
some small part to peel away.

On Sundays
he cleans his house with a feather duster
so not to disturb
his things too much

but alas.
Once we didn't feel the earth turn either.

*

This eon will end
without us
unfurl its woven grass mat down a hundred-mile beach
and spark a brand-new thing.

Imagine how pristine
what's next.
No narrator.
No corps of engineers.
No one to jump
through the fire and bend it.

IV

Decades

whose name won't be lost?

Spiraling in the absence

of god and wedged
between the holocaust and a morning glory
a friend asked me in a coffee shop
if I believed in the equality of all conditions
to which I flicked a sugar cube
across the checkerboard floor
where it bounced until it stopped
on the border between countries.

But that was three decades ago.
And now, double-parked
under the influence of each of them
I think what he meant to say was
In the end, do you suppose there's nothing more
than an even distribution of the elements?

Peals of laughter from the next table
stopped the live birth of those words
and the coffee in our saucers
and the cool-jazz soundtrack
stopped us from sculpting
a concept anywhere near that grand
bound as we were
by law to follow
the arc of our waitress from behind
who drifted
like silk on silk.

Old Lady Painter

We gathered around the ambulance
in front of my neighbor's house
to see what was going on.

Her son came out to tell us.
He said magnetism had kept her
from tumbling over the balcony for years
but it just couldn't hold her
back anymore.

He said she was a raven, old-lady painter
working behind a row of windows.
Trees moved across her pages, he said.
Her pages moved among the trees.

In the still unwritten
part of this poem
which is really just
my godless prayer for her
a stranger finds her folio
twenty years later in a thrift store
takes it home
and hangs her faded pages
on the clothesline in his mind.

Street Vendor Florist

She wheels under a blue tarp
turning what she finds
in a customer's face
into blooms and greenery
using what she has
an eye for and a blur
of steel to snip
the dead parts away
until what's left
is the bare essence of love
reduced to a delicate grief
nestled in a web of baby's breath.

For ten dollars a customer gets
the same bouquet as the customer before him
but doesn't care.
I know someone who'd love those white ones
I say, pointing behind her.
But she doesn't look
where I pointed
owning my eyes forever instead.

Thus these hobbled words.

Although Much is Implied

There's plenty of time left
to reinvent myself today
get a haircut and power-wash something.

I go to the public library
and thumb through the '62 World Book
Encyclopedia for ideas
to see what tools I'll need, what workbench.

The section on Soviet industrial output is eye-catching
but sad, so no.
The part on tungsten…just no.
But look: The air force launched a satellite.
So...maybe that?

I can't find a thing that shows how to make love
generate an income
although much is implied.
And it's obvious the future belongs to playwrights
physicists and soybeans.
So…maybe one of those?

The librarian offers to help me
find a town that needs a five-and-dime
or a tower that needs a bell.
That's sweet of you, I tell her, *but don't worry
something always bubbles up.*

In '62, a girl down the street got a trampoline.
We jumped the hell out of it that summer
and later each other.
So, I'm thinking…maybe that?

Not once in a decade

have I seen someone in the brittle graveyard near my house.

It must be easy at first
sitting cross-legged before a clean new stone
to strip the bark off a stick
catch a whiff of the flame puffed out
and pour your bloody heart out to it.

But maybe everything a stone can hear
can be said in an hour
and by the second visit we're not so sure
we caught as much tart wisp
of smoke as we first thought.

Atoms replace atoms
and memories migrate to the dreamscape
which means they're in a box in the shed
with the favorite sweater and the last-read book
waiting to be dropped off at the thrift store.

The dead can't spark
a pale finger back to life
no matter how hard we ask.
And by the time the sugar maple at the cemetery gate
flames on and off
naked for the season
maybe there's nothing left to visit

just some grass along the fence line
where the mower couldn't reach.

In December '44, in the Ardennes,

you fired a tripod
machine gun into snow
until a German bullet broke
your helmet and gave you something
big to dream about.
When your ears stopped ringing
summer returned
and you turned twenty-three
in Paris.
Headlines tore the papers open,
Unconditional Surrender
De Gaulle's frail voice
falling from gangly speakers
strung up in the square.
And so your year-long occupation began.
Turkish cigarettes, beer and local girls
love letters passing at sea.
You zigzagged the continent's patched-up rails
following orders, taking up space
until a transport floated you
vaguely home to Cincinnati.
On the train from New York
whistle stops
gave you all the time you needed
to pick stars off the men
who sent you there.
You bounded down the broom-swept steps
at Cincinnati's Union Station
in a hurry to stand at the vaulted altar.
Twelve months asleep in the law library
bought you a degree
four sons and a corporate black hole.
Decades flew

off your fingers like sparks
off a cartwheel firework.
You were the one foretold
the one your German ancestors'
own Atlantic passage guaranteed.
But before all that
before the mortarboard and baptisms
before paychecks and holiday dinners
before kids and packed ashtrays
stuttered your heart
back in November '46 to be exact
perched on the fulcrum between
what was and would be
a month before your wedding
you wrote in a letter to your future wife
If I'm alive in '99, I'll still love you
a letter revealed in my hands now
your full-slant longhand
still falling forward
the ink sill blue after seventy years
the envelope you sealed and addressed
its deep-sky postmark like a guardian moon
your lost face in my hands.

for Danny

1952-2017

Last night I dreamed we were kids again.
We sat by a window looking out
in awe at plastic space.
I handed you a prism
and when you held it up to the light
color streamed across your face.
Do you remember?

In '69, a heavy rain broke
and the dam at Franklin Lake washed away.
We switched from climbing trees
to losing shoes in muck.
The lake-bed was like Mars to us
still steaming a month later
secrets exposed, melting away.

The grasses grew back first
then the seedlings
then a full-blown rupture of life ensued.

How memory's light scrubs the old air clean.

I've decided to remember you
only in childhood from now on if I can
when the air was fit to breathe
and the sky was plastered with stars
and we passed through the years of discovery together.

What to Expect of the Decades

—for a three-year-old boy who hasn't asked yet—

*

The first ten years are up to chance.
The color of your eyes and the smell of your skin.
Riding your parents' topography.

You and your avatar go places.
People give you candy.
Everything goes without a hitch
until one day you make the mistake
of saving a seedling maple from the lawnmower.

You couldn't have guessed it would take forever
to learn everything it knows.

*

In your teens, you take a rain check
at your local school for the gullibly insane.
They don't allow your kind
of humor there anyway
encrypted obtuse with a touch of Chaplin.

You climb a tree with high-hanging fruit
and become an anthropologist.

Then, one winter, she finds you
the girl from nowhere.
Warm as a sauna beside the frozen lake.
The ice that year
thin enough to skate on.

*

In your 20s, you pass through a sunrise
to see what colors are like
on the other side.

You stick your stubbly chin out
re-toss the dice
write on the back of a postcard to yourself
It's either a particle or a wave.

You, the provocateur photographer
bumming your way across Europe
reflected in a train-car window.

On the Rome to Amsterdam
a woman offers you half a peach
stuck on the end of a paring knife.

Everyone else is asleep
she whispers.

*

In your 30s, you work around your work
to give the Daddy-years permission.

The rotation nearly catches up with itself.
Your kids' favorite songs compose themselves on the piano.
No one interrupts when someone is singing.

In the back yard, on the path between
the rhody and the vine-maple
a bird's nest, high up.

You call in sick to build a perch
to watch and wonder from.
Three blue eggs. Dappled shade. Snacks.

*

If you're lucky, your 40s are a feedlot
for your swollen assets
but you have to know which stars to thank.

Look into your contractor's eyes.
When he snaps his fingers
you'll reveal what species of deck-wood you want
what grade shingles.

One day there's a hold-up
at the front of the check-out line.
You mutter something unkind.
Behind tinted glasses
no one can see what an epitaph you've become.

*

It's best to float
down the entire length of your 50s
in an innertube, wrap your arms around

passing compass points and squeeze
until the heavy ones sink and the light ones disappear.
Equilibrium up close, true or not
helps you focus.

If a wino floats by, ignore him.
If a suicide bomber floats by, ignore him.

Even god doesn't know
what's in the water.
The book you write is in the water.

*

In your 60s, you forget the point behind
your expensive landscaping.
You like the fallen leaves
where they fall now.
Pumpkin scones for the neighbors
you walk barefoot, off-sidewalk, to deliver them
to feel the earth's ribs connect
with the jungle in your feet.

Blended seasons somehow.
Air: cool *and* warm.
Sky: blue *and* pink.

All that talk about moving to Rome
is ancient history now.

*

At the end of your 70s
you remember being five
aboard The Maid of the Mist at Niagara.

Huddled under your mother's plastic poncho
the blast of the falls your first true calm
inside a storm.

Every morning now you take a long walk
for your health.
When you get home
on the hallway table
acorns and sticks
pinecones and leaves.

About the Author

John Harn grew up in Michigan, spent his adult life in Oregon and wrote most of these poems in Galveston. For thirty years he worked with adult international students in a variety of roles including ESL teaching, curriculum design, program administration, student advising, and college admissions. His first full-length collection, *Physics for Beginners,* won the 2017 Blue Light Press Book Award and was published that year in San Francisco. His poems have been in Carolina Quarterly, Chicago Quarterly, Denver Quarterly, Hotel Amerika, Miramar, New Orleans Review, Pleiades, Poetry East, Post Road, Prairie Schooner, South Carolina Review, Cloudbank, Spillway, and other journals. He has an MFA in Poetry from the University of Oregon and has taught poetry writing at the University of Oregon, Pacific University (in Oregon) and at the Oregon State Penitentiary. He's the co-author of three daughters and a Grampa to Abe.

Kelsay Books
(Aldrich Press)

www.ingramcontent.com/pod-product-compliance
Lightning Source LLC
Chambersburg PA
CBHW031928080426
42734CB00007B/595